PANORAMAS
DINOSAURS

BACKPACKBOOKS

○

NEW YORK

CONTENTS

THE DINOSAURS' DESCENDANTS

The first birds evolved during the Age of Dinosaurs. Archaeopteryx, which lived in Europe around 150 million years ago, was one of the earliest birds known from the fossil record. It had a tooth-filled beak, a long, bony tail, and feathers. It lived in the same place and at the same time as the tiny, fast-running dinosaur, Compsognathus. The skeletons of the two animals were very similar, leading scientists to think that Archaeopteryx evolved from dinosaurs.

CETIOSAURUS

BRACHIOSAURUS

THE WORLD OF THE DINOSAURS

DINOSAURS ruled the world for more than 160 million years. While they were around, no other large land animals existed. Some kinds, the massive long-necked dinosaurs, were the largest animals that ever walked on land. Others, such as Tyrannosaurus rex, were the most powerful carnivores of all time. Not for nothing were these reptiles given the name that means "terrible lizards."

CETIOSAURUS

EUSTREPTOSPONDYLUS

PROCERATOSAURUS

Some fish developed proper limbs with fingers and toes, becoming the first amphibians. These animals still kept close to water, where they laid their jelly-covered eggs. Some creatures found a way to lay eggs on land. They were the first reptiles.

RISE OF THE REPTILES

From the late Carboniferous period and on into the Permian, reptiles spread to all parts of the world. They could lay eggs on land, so they were able to live almost anywhere, including lands with dry climates. The baby reptiles were protected by a shell and had yolk for food. New kinds of reptiles developed strong legs, tough skin, and powerful jaws that they used to bite on flesh and plants.

KEY

1 Eusthenopteron
2 Hylonomus
3 Dragonfly
4 Eryops

5 Dimetrodon
6 Scutosaurus
7 Moschops
8 Coelurosauravus

PERMIAN

245 million years ago

THE RISE OF THE DINOSAURS

MORE THAN 360 million years ago, in the Devonian period, warm tropical waters lapped the shores of places like Scotland and Canada. Some large, bony fish that lived there evolved lungs and fleshy fins, and could stay out of the water for a while.

DEVONIAN

360 million years ago

CARBONIFEROUS

286 million years ago

WHAT WERE DINOSAURS?

DINOSAURS were land reptiles that stood with their legs beneath their bodies, like mammals and birds do today. Neither marine reptiles nor flying reptiles were dinosaurs, although they lived during the same age. The legs of most reptiles, like modern-day lizards, are at the side of their bodies. Thecodonts were prehistoric reptiles that had partly bent legs. Some of the thecodonts may have evolved into the first dinosaurs.

KOMODO DRAGON (LIZARD)

THECODONT

DINOSAUR

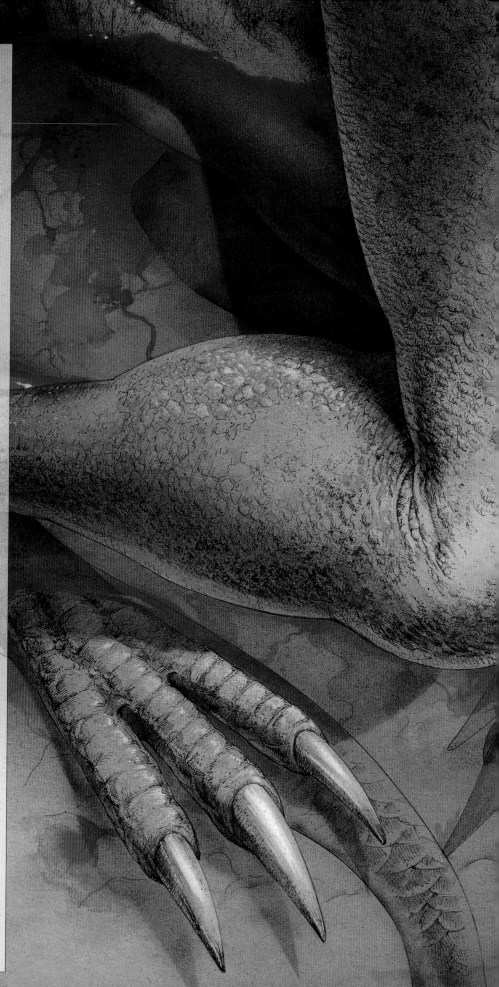

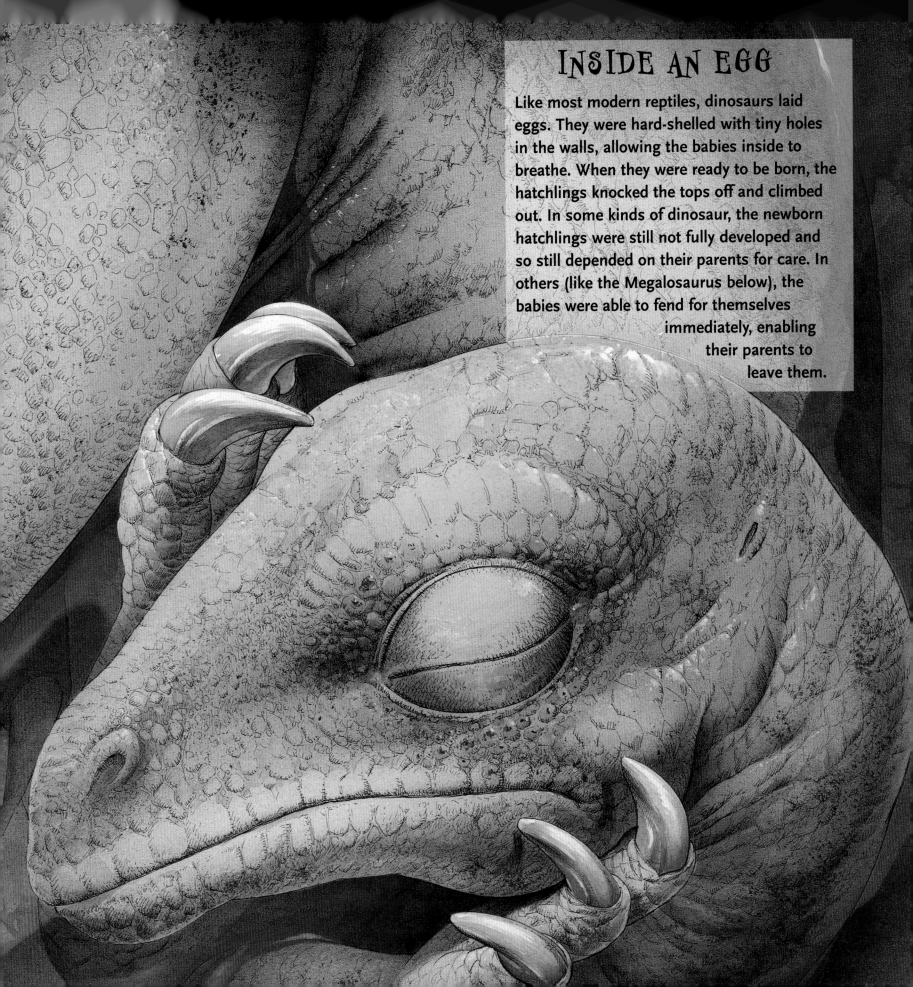

INSIDE AN EGG

Like most modern reptiles, dinosaurs laid eggs. They were hard-shelled with tiny holes in the walls, allowing the babies inside to breathe. When they were ready to be born, the hatchlings knocked the tops off and climbed out. In some kinds of dinosaur, the newborn hatchlings were still not fully developed and so still depended on their parents for care. In others (like the Megalosaurus below), the babies were able to fend for themselves immediately, enabling their parents to leave them.

JURASSIC GIANTS

Most of the story of the dinosaurs takes place during two geological periods: the Jurassic and Cretaceous. The Jurassic was the heyday of the truly gigantic sauropods, like Diplodocus. Their very size may have saved them from fierce predators like Allosaurus, seen here about to devour a slightly smaller sauropod, Camarasaurus.

FLYING REPTILES

Before the Jurassic period, only insects had conquered the air. Now, pterosaurs, the first true flying vertebrates, soared in the skies. By the late Cretaceous they were huge hunters: some were the size of small planes!

KEY

24 Camarasaurus

25 Iguanodon   29 Quetzalcoatlus

26 Corythosaurus   30 Struthiomimus

27 Styracosaurus   31 Magnolia

28 Tyrannosaurus   32 Morganucodon

144 million years ago

CRETACEOUS

65 million years ago

KEY

9 Lystrosaurus
10 Proterosuchus
11 Ornithosuchus
12 Coelophysis
13 Plateosaurus
14 Phytosaur
15 Proganochelys
   (turtle)
16 Eudimorphodon

17 Megazostrodon
18 Dilophosaurus
19 Diplodocus
20 Archaeopteryx
21 Pterodactylus
22 Brachiosaurus
23 Allosaurus

AGE OF DINOSAURS

By the Triassic period, some reptiles were standing upright and getting about on two legs: the dinosaurs had arrived. The first dinosaurs were flesh eaters. They had long, powerful back legs for running and short arms with claws for grappling. Some later flesh eaters were massive. Others were small sprinters no bigger than cats.

TRIASSIC

208 million years ago

JURASSIC

ATTACK AND DEFENSE

THE FLESH-EATING dinosaurs, known as theropods, ran about on their two hind legs. Large theropods probably hunted or scavenged alone, while smaller ones may have worked in packs.

Although they were much smaller dinosaurs, several Eustreptospondylus together could have launched an attack on a massive Cetiosaurus. The predators would circle their chosen victim warily, watching it very carefully, as it could be dangerous when threatened.

If they were able to dodge its defenses, the hunters would rush at their prey, using their claws and teeth to bring it down.

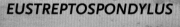

EUSTREPTOSPONDYLUS

CETIOSAURUS

BACK OFF!

Cetiosaurus was a very sturdy sauropod, one of a number of long-necked plant-eating dinosaurs that lived during the Jurassic period. Its spoon-shaped teeth were perfect for tearing off tree leaves. Like many sauropods, it would have roamed around in herds, relying on strength of numbers as a means of defense. But, if attacked, it could still defend itself very ably. For what it lacked in speed, Cetiosaurus made up for in sheer size. It could rear up on its back legs and crash down on its attackers. It may also have flicked its whiplike tail with great force into the predators' faces.

IGUANODON

30 feet long Early Cretaceous
Europe, Asia, North America

Iguanodon was one of the first dinosaurs to be discovered and studied. Iguanodon probably walked on all fours, rearing up on its pillarlike hind legs to run at high speed, to feed on leaves up in the trees, or to unleash its viciously sharp thumb spike to defend itself from predators.

TRICERATOPS

30 feet long Late Cretaceous
North America

The best-known horned dinosaur, Triceratops (meaning "three-horned face"), was also the largest and commonest member of its family. It lived right at the end of the dinosaur era, at the same time as Tyrannosaurus rex. A frill of solid bone protected its neck, while its long, sharp horns equipped it for attack.

CRESTS AND SPIKES

Some dinosaurs, such as Parasaurolophus and Lambeosaurus, had crests on top of their heads. These were made of solid bone. The tubes inside may have amplified their calls. Pachycephalosaurus's domed head may have been used in head-butting contests between males. Armored dinosaurs, such as Euoplocephalus, were protected by a covering of bony slabs, studs, and spikes. Stegosaurus had long spikes on its tail that it could have swung in the face of attackers.

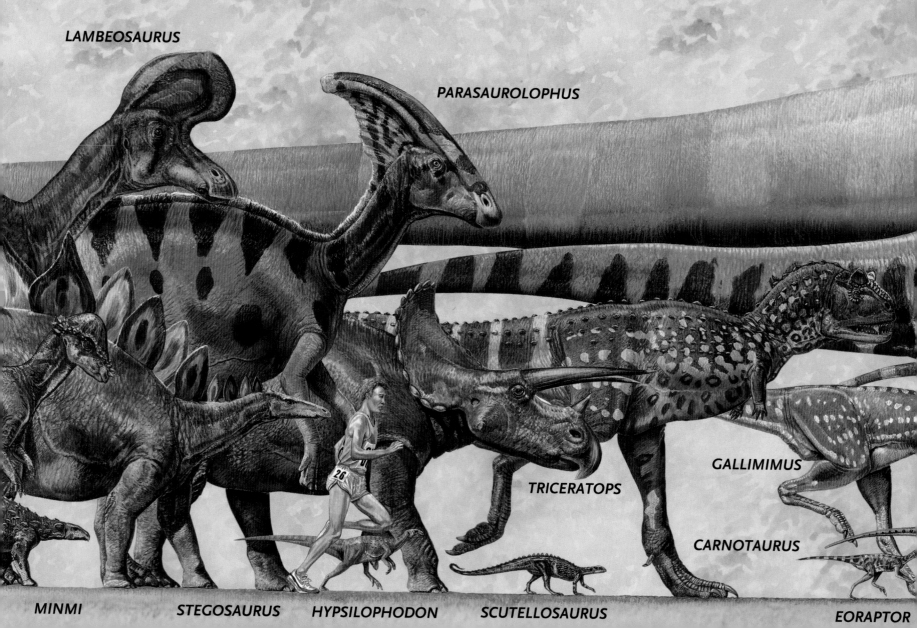

LAMBEOSAURUS

PARASAUROLOPHUS

GALLIMIMUS

TRICERATOPS

CARNOTAURUS

MINMI   STEGOSAURUS   THYPSILOPHODON   SCUTELLOSAURUS   EORAPTOR

DINOSAUR SPECIES

DINOSAURS formed two major groups: the saurischians ("lizard hipped"), whose hip bones were shaped like those of other reptiles, and the ornithischians ("bird hipped"), whose hip bones were like those of modern birds—although birds are, in fact, descendants of saurischian rather than ornithischian dinosaurs. Both the theropods (flesh eaters) and the long-necked sauropods were saurischians. The ornithischian group included the hadrosaurs, ceratopsians, stegosaurs, and ankylosaurs.

All we know about dinosaurs has been learned from the study of their fossilized remains, including bones, teeth, droppings, and eggs. Impressions of skin, feathers, and footprints have also provided vital clues for scientists. Although these may not be enough for us to re-create a dinosaur's exact appearance or color, such evidence taken together with what we know about the behavior of modern animals can still tell us a lot about how dinosaurs lived.

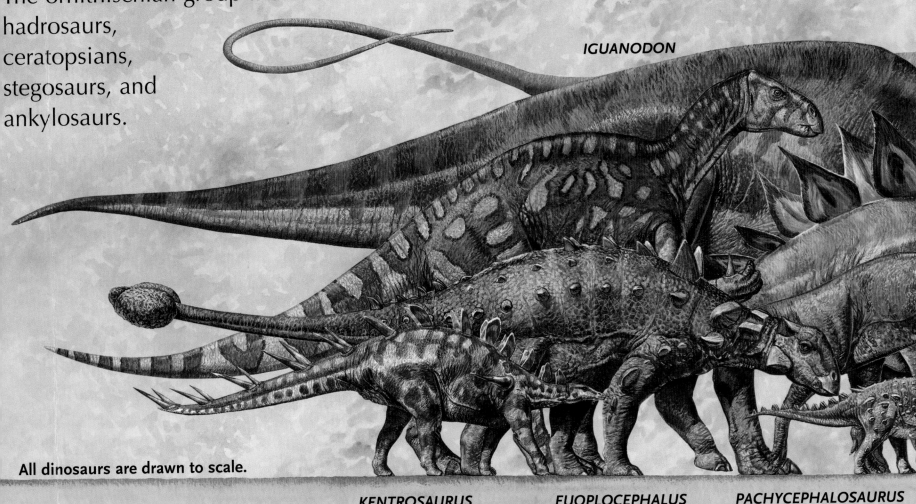

IGUANODON

All dinosaurs are drawn to scale.

KENTROSAURUS   *EUOPLOCEPHALUS*   *PACHYCEPHALOSAURUS*

THE LIFE OF A DINOSAUR

MAMENCHISAURUS was a sauropod that lived in China 160 million years ago. It was one of the longest-necked dinosaurs of all: an adult dinosaur grew up to 80 feet long. But, like all dinosaurs, it started life as an egg only a couple of inches in size. Females laid their eggs in nests scooped out of the soil.

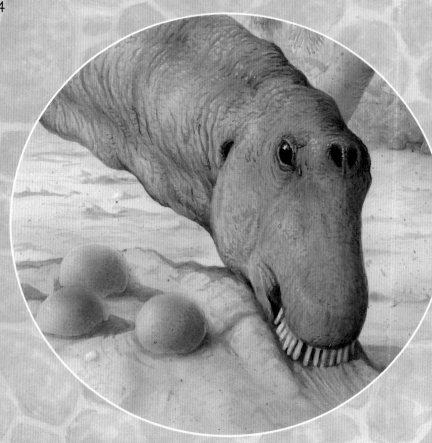

A NESTING COLONY

The mother uses her teeth to rake the soil into a small mound around her eggs. She guards the eggs against other, smaller dinosaurs that threaten to steal them. When they hatch out, her young are only 15 inches long.

YOUNG DINOSAURS

The young Mamenchisaurus grow up quickly on a diet of ferns and other plants. Despite being cared for by their parents, many of these young dinosaurs will fall prey to flesh-eating dinosaurs before they become adults. Only when they are several feet long will they be able to roam and feed on leaves and needles from the trees themselves.

ON THE MOVE

Like some plant-eating animals today, many sauropods, probably including Mamenchisaurus, lived in herds. They found extra protection in numbers. Some male members would have fought one another to be the leader of the herd.

As the dry season sets in and the vegetation dies back, this herd of Mamenchisaurus sets out for greener forests and swamps hundreds of miles away. The young walk in the center of the herd while the adults keep a look-out for danger.

FLASH FLOOD

The dinosaurs have so far avoided attack by predatory dinosaurs such as the fearsome Yangchuanosaurus. But they have fallen foul of stormy weather. While they cross a ravine, the stream suddenly becomes a raging torrent. One of the Mamenchisaurus is overpowered by the force of the flood and drowns. Its body sinks to the bottom of the water, where it is immediately covered over by mud and silt.

PRESERVED IN STONE

The process of fossilization now begins. Over millions of years, the mud and silt slowly turn to rock. Meanwhile, water with minerals dissolved in it seeps into the pores, or tiny holes, inside the bones. Gradually the bones are replaced by the minerals and become part of the surrounding rock. The exact shape of the original skeleton is preserved. Perhaps in years to come, the rocks will be exposed above ground and the fossil will be discovered.

GIGANTIC GRAZERS

Sauropods fed on tough conifer needles. They would rake them from the trees with their teeth, using their long necks to reach high up into the treetops. Their teeth could not chew the needles so they swallowed stones called gastroliths, which helped to grind up the needles in their guts. Sauropods needed huge stomachs to hold the vast quantity of food they consumed.

SEISMOSAURUS

130 feet long Late Jurassic North America

Members of the diplodocid family were the longest dinosaurs. Diplodocus itself is the longest known dinosaur from a complete skeleton (90 feet), but comparisons made from the few bones so far discovered of its relative Seismosaurus suggest that this giant may have been much longer—about the width of a football field! Much of its length was made up of its long neck and whiplike tail.

AMARGASAURUS

30 feet long Cretaceous South America

The fossil remains of this unusual sauropod were discovered in Argentina. Amargasaurus had long spines pointing backward from the top of its neck. Horn-covered and with sharp tips, they probably stood out from the skin (as illustrated here) and were used in defense. Amargasaurus's lethal mane would have protected its neck from the ferocious jaws of its predators.

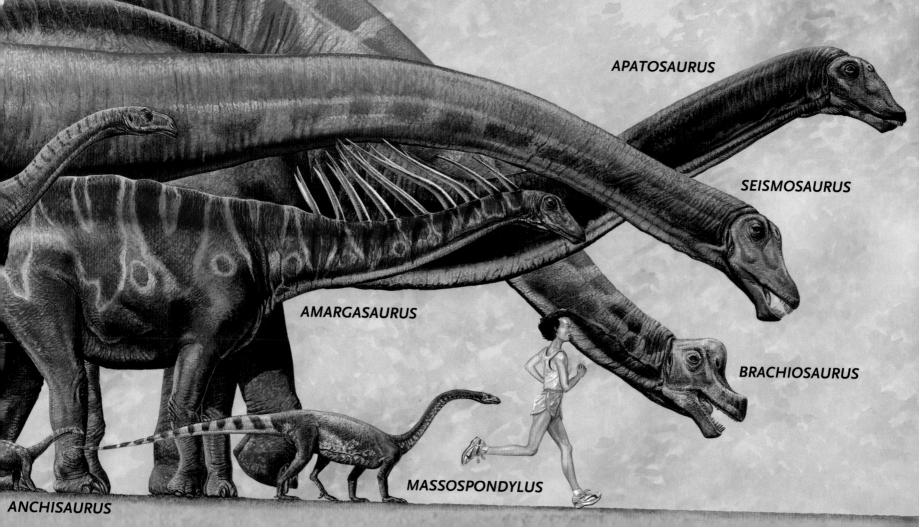

APATOSAURUS

SEISMOSAURUS

AMARGASAURUS

BRACHIOSAURUS

MASSOSPONDYLUS

ANCHISAURUS

TYRANNOSAURUS REX

*40 feet long Late Cretaceous
North America*

Tyrannosaurus rex was one of the largest and most powerful flesh-eating animals ever to walk the Earth. Longer than the width of a doubles tennis court, it would have towered above humans— were they to have lived in the same age. An eight-year old child could have stood in its gaping mouth, surrounded by rows of saw-edged teeth, some up to 7 inches long and each the size and sharpness of a butcher's knife. Its tiny, two-fingered arms were too short to bring food to its mouth. Relying on its keen senses of sight, smell, and hearing, Tyrannosaurus may have hunted by ambushing its prey: waiting stealthily before rushing at its victim with gaping jaws.

ALLOSAURUS

*35 feet long Late Jurassic
North America, East Africa, Australia*

In its time Allosaurus was without rival for size and ferocity. Hunting in packs, this animal was big enough to bring down most of the great sauropods. It had three big clawed toes with a shorter fourth toe behind, and backward-curving teeth that would have made it difficult for prey to struggle free from its jaws!

TYRANNOSAURUS REX

ALLOSAURUS

OVIRAPTOR

UTAHRAPTOR   COMPSOGNATHUS   VELOCIRAPTOR   PLATEOSAURUS

WHAT HAPPENED TO THE DINOSAURS?

ABOUT 65 million years ago, the dinosaurs were gone. There are no more fossils of dinosaurs after this time, the end of the Cretaceous period. The dinosaurs were not alone in becoming extinct. Sea reptiles, such as ichthyosaurs and plesiosaurs, also disappeared. So did the pterosaurs, along with many kinds of shellfish in the oceans and large numbers of plants. Three-quarters of life on Earth vanished forever. What caused this terrible disaster?

METEORITE

Many scientists think that a massive asteroid—a large rocky object in space—may have crashed into Earth at this time, punching a large crater and throwing up huge quantities of dust high into the atmosphere. The sun would have been blotted out, lowering temperatures for years on end. Massive volcanic eruptions could have produced the same effect.

DEATH OF THE DINOSAURS

No one knows what caused the dinosaurs to die out, or why other kinds of animals survived. It may have been that the dinosaurs were already in decline, and that colder climates, possibly brought about by years of continuous volcanic eruptions or bombardment by meteorites, finished them off.

MAMMALS

In this scene, scavenging birds circle overhead while small mammals arrive to pick the bones of a dead Triceratops. Although mammals had first appeared millions of years earlier, they lived through the Age of Dinosaurs as tiny, nocturnal, shrewlike animals. Now their time had come.

WHO SURVIVED?

While the dinosaurs, along with marine and flying reptiles, perished at the end of the Cretaceous period, other reptiles, including lizards, snakes, turtles, and crocodiles, survived. Mammals also lived on. Birds, which had descended from small feathered dinosaurs and first evolved in the Jurassic, were also survivors.

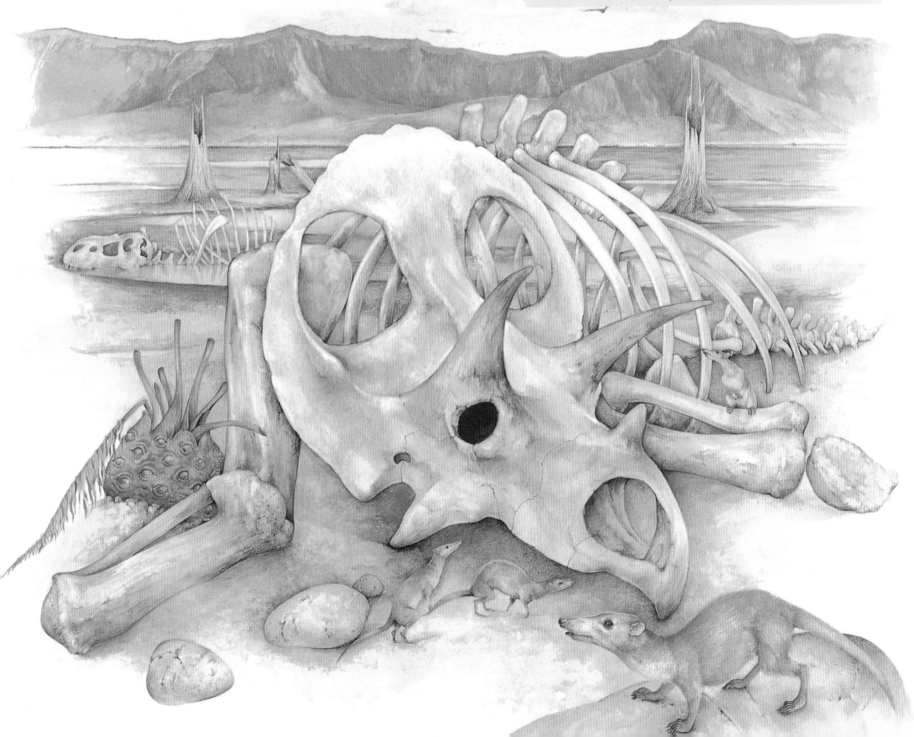

GLOSSARY

ANKYLOSAURS Ornithischian dinosaurs fully covered in armored plates, studs, and spikes. Some, like Euoplocephalus, had tail clubs.

CERATOPSIANS Horned dinosaurs of the ornithischian type. Some, like Triceratops, had huge neck frills and narrow beaks.

DINOSAURS Reptiles that lived on land 250-65 million years ago and walked upright on legs held beneath their bodies.

DIPLODOCIDS Sauropod dinosaurs with long, slender bodies, and tails. They include Diplodocus, Apatosaurus, and Seismosaurus.

EVOLUTION The process by which forms of life change. Animals and plants may **evolve** over millions of years, gradually adapting to make the best use of their environment.

FOSSIL The remains of an animal or plant preserved in rock. A living thing becomes **fossilized** when it is buried by sediments and the spaces within its tissues are filled by minerals that set hard over time.

HADROSAURS "Duck-billed" dinosaurs from the late Cretaceous period. Grazing in herds, they were plant eaters with grinding teeth.

ICHTHYOSAURS Marine reptiles with a dolphinlike shape and long flippers.

ORNITHISCHIANS The "bird-hipped" dinosaurs, one of two major types of dinosaur. Ornithischians had backward-slanting pubic bones—the lower part of the hip bone.

PLESIOSAURS Marine reptiles with long necks, small heads, and large, paddlelike flippers.

PTEROSAURS Flying reptiles with wings that were formed from skin flaps between their fourth finger and lower body.

SAURISCHIANS The "lizard-hipped"' dinosaurs, one of two major types of dinosaur. Saurischians had forward-jutting pubic bones—the lower part of the hip bone.

SAUROPODS Long-necked, four-legged, plant-eating dinosaurs. They were the very largest and heaviest land animals of all time.

STEGOSAURS Plated dinosaurs of the ornithischian type. They had rows of plates and spikes embedded in their backs.

THEROPODS All the meat-eating saurischian dinosaurs.